Minnie Gilmore

Pipes from Prairie-Land, and other places

Minnie Gilmore

Pipes from Prairie-Land, and other places

ISBN/EAN: 9783743328525

Manufactured in Europe, USA, Canada, Australia, Japa

Cover: Foto ©ninafisch / pixelio.de

Manufactured and distributed by brebook publishing software (www.brebook.com)

Minnie Gilmore

Pipes from Prairie-Land, and other places

COPYRIGHT, 1886,
BY O. M. DUNHAM.

PRESS OF HUNTER & BEACH,
NEW YORK.

CONTENTS.

	PAGE
PRELUDE	7

PIPES FROM PRAIRIE-LAND.

WATOOSKA	11
THE SHOOTING STAR	22
THE RIVER ON THE PLAIN	25
A PRAIRIE FLOWER	30
JUANITA	32
A WESTERN WEDDING	34
AN AUTUMN CANTER	39
MOWING THE HARVEST HAY	42
ATTUNED	44
THE HUSKING OF THE CORN	46

CONTENTS.

The Deserted Cabin . . . .
A Sorghum Candy-Pull . . . .

IN THE ORIGINAL KEY.

A Pioneer Poet . . . . . .
Dare-Devil Dick . . . .
A Border Romance . . . .
At the Mouth of the Tunnel . . . . .
While the White Corn Pops . . . . .
An Open Letter . . . . . .
Jim . . . .
Transplanted . . . .
Blackbird . . . .

PIPES FROM OTHER PLACES.

A Quintette of Song: I.—Life . . . . .
    II.—Love . . . .
    III.—Song . . . .
    IV.—Peace . . . . . .
    V.—Death . . . .
Cleo . . . .
After the Ball . . . .

CONTENTS.

	PAGE
Three Serenades: I.	118
II.	119
III.	120
By the River	122
Fall Harbingers	123
On the Hill	124
The Deserted Chapel	127
To the Rain	129
The Wind	132
A Snow Song	134
The Lesson of the Crucifix	136
A Virgin Chaplet	139
A Lamp for the Tabernacle	142
Adieu	144

CODA.

| To my Critics | 149 |

PRELUDE.

THE sun sails down to the west.
*   O friends! let us drift in its wake,*
To the mountains with snowy crest,
To the canyons hung high with brake;
To the pine-trees that bend and blow;
To the copses where roses hide,
And the streams that run swift beside.–
O friends, let us go, let us go!

The wind blows down to the west.
O friends! let us follow its flight,
To the crags where the eaglets nest,
And the phantom-braves flit by night;
To the prairies that gleam below,
Where the buffaloes run at will,
And the prairie-dog mounts his hill.—
O friends, let us go, let us go!

The birds fly down to the west.
O friends! let us flee in their train,

PRELUDE.

To the wigwams that frown abreast,
To the towns on the lonely plain;
To the farms where the milch-cows low,
Where the horses in pastures play,
And the meadows are sweet with hay.—
O friends, let us go, let us go!

The dusk drifts down to the west.
O friends, let us speed in its trail,
To the life that is free and best,
To the folk that are blithe and hale;
To the kindly hearts that I know,
To the hearth of the pioneer,
To the simple and cordial cheer.—
O friends, let us go, let us go!

The gold stars break in the west.
O friends, that my pipes so might soar,
Stars of song, from the fair young breast
Of our beautiful western shore!
Warm and red as the flashing Mars,
They should beck you and draw you on
To the "Land of the Setting Sun"—
O friends, were my songs but as stars!

PIPES FROM PRAIRIE-LAND.

WATOOSKA.

NORTH from the sunny Great Water,
    The far Mississippi—
North from Otope, the alders,
    The singing, wet valley—
Far in the land of the Red Man,
    The shadowy Northland,
Glimmers a forest of pine trees,
    Still, dusky as twilight.
There, 'mid the silence and shadows,
    There, long years gone over,
Rounded through springtimes and summers,
    A live bud to flower,
Bloom of the blood of the Red Man,
    The breast of the Pale-face;
Born of the chief and his captive,
    Watooska, White Lily.

Two races battled within her,
    Warred in her young bosom;

PIPES FROM PRAIRIE-LAND.

Two natures played on her heartstrings,
    Flamed hot in her pulses,
Mingled within her their hatreds,
    Their loves and their passions.
Loved she the old chief, her father,
    Megizze, White Eagle;
Loved in him all the fierce Red Men,
    Her savage, wild people;
Loved the pinewoods, and the wigwam,
    The glowing feast torches;
Loved her dead mother, the Pale-face,
    The gentle, white captive—
Loved for her sake all her kindred,
    The foe, the Pale-faces.

Fairest of all the Ojibway
    Fair maidens, Watooska.
Fair, slim, and supple as Kezhik,
    Kezhik, the white cedar;
Lissom and swift as the robin,
    The lissom Opechee.
Eyes of brown depths, wide and plaintive
    As eyes of the reindeer;
Lashes more dark than Kahgahgee,
    More dark than the raven.

PIPES FROM PRAIRIE-LAND.

Up the white cheek of her mother,
    The cheek of the Pale-face,
Crimson the blood of Megizze,
    The Red Man, the chieftain.
Sweet her soft voice, as the falling,
    Far, light Minnehaha.

Oft' to the door of her wigwam
    Sped young braves, her lovers;
Sped in their warpaint and feathers,
    With wampum and trophies;
Runners, and wrestlers, and dancers,
    And rulers, and warriors;
Hunters with slings and with arrows,
    Game warm on their shoulders;
Sued all in vain for Watooska,
    In vain for White Lily;
Thus ever chanting Megizze:—
    "Be it as thy heart wilt.
Say thou, yea, nay, O my daughter,
    Say thou, my Watooska!"
"Nay, then, my father!" in answer,
    With soft voice, White Lily.

Why did she sigh as she answered,
    Tears bright on her eyelids?

PIPES FROM PRAIRIE-LAND.

Why wandered ever at twilight,
    Hands clasped in her tresses,
Dusky eyes blinded with anguish,
    Lips spent with long moaning,
Out from the lodge and the maidens,
    The braves and young chieftains,
Out from the fires and the dances,
    The tales and the feasting,
Up to the rim of the forest,
    The lonely, far mountain—
Up to the crag crowned with pine trees,
    To fling herself headlong
Down by its brink, fierce eyes piercing
    The still deeps below it?

Ah, here her lover had wooed her,
    Here, here, he had won her!—
Pale Chief, the young Wabishkizzi,
    The daring young Pale-face.
Braved at the hands of the Red Men
    Slow death by sore torture,
Stake, and sure knife, and fleet arrow,
    Through one sweet, warm summer;
Sped out at night from the village,
    Spurs deep in his courser,

PIPES FROM PRAIRIE-LAND.

Swift as the wind, to the fragrant
    West rim of the forest;
Flung on low branches the bridle,
    And stole, silent-footed,
Up through the trees to the tryst-place—
    Up, up, to Watooska.

Here 'neath the stars he had wooed her,
    Had wooed her and won her;
Here, to the rim of the forest,
    The lonely, far mountain,
Here, to the crag crowned with pine trees,
    One languid, late twilight,
Stealthy and sure as the panther,
    One stilly had tracked him,
Jealous, mad hate in his bosom;
    Sped out from the shadows
Lithe as a flame, from his quiver
    A hissing, sure arrow;
Harking the cry of Watooska,
    As over the crag-brink,
Down the lone fathoms her lover,
    Smote by the Great Spirit.

What saw the dim-eyed Megizze,
    As back to her wigwam,

PIPES FROM PRAIRIE-LAND.

Wan as a wraith, stole the maiden,
    Chill, mute as the midnight—
That from the threshold he lifted
    The furry, soft curtain,
Bade her pass in all unchidden,
    And slumber till daybreak?
That through the night he sat musing
    Alone at his doorway,
Flame in his pipe fading palely,
    Unfed and forgotten—
Thence, when her lovers besought her,
    Bade ever in answer:
"Say thou, yea, nay, O my daughter,
    Say thou, my Watooska?"—

That when round moons, ripe and ruddy,
    A half score had faded—
When, o'er the Ottawa warcry
    That rang from the lodges,
Chusco, first-born of Ningwegon,
    Great Ottawa chieftain,
Holding the pipe to Megizze,
    Said, "Give me thy daughter!
Give me Watooska, and ended
    The warfare and bloodshed!"

PIPES FROM PRAIRIE-LAND.

Torn with his love for his people,
    The threatened Ojibways—
Yearning the peace-pipe, Megizze
    Yet gently waived answer:—
"Say thou, yea, nay, O my daughter,
    Say thou, my Watooska?"

Out to the crag crowned with pine trees,
    That dusk, sped Watooska;
Waged through the twilight and midnight
    Fierce war with her spirit;
Wrestled alone, empty-handed,
    Palms clenched on the crag-brink,
Writhing in mortal, mute anguish,
    Lips set; hot eyes tearless.
Rose up at daybreak: "Forgive me,
    Forgive me," she pleaded;
"Sweetheart, my dead Wabishkizzi—
    Forgive me, O Pale-face!
Thou my one love, O my lover,
    My one love forever!"
Sought then, Megizze, and faltered,
    "As thou wilt, my father."

Great then, the joy of Megizze,
    The rapture of Chusco;

PIPES FROM PRAIRIE-LAND.

Lightsome the hearts of her people,
    The ransomed Ojibways.
Out from the Ottawa lodges
    In peace came the foemen,
Young braves and dauntless old chieftains,
    And rulers and warriors,
Painted and plumed for the bridal,
    The feast and the peace-pipe.
Happy the squaws and old women
    Grouped round on the rushes;
Gleeful the youths and brown maidens,
    Fawn-fleet in the dances;
Laughing the swart young pappooses;—
    Sad only Watooska.

Palely from height of the feasting
    She stole to the shadows;
Soft in her footprints sped Chusco,
    Her lover, her husband;
Heat more than love in his pulses,
    The burning fire-water
Spur to his savage, fierce spirit,
    His passion, his triumph.
What did his fevered word whisper
    That smote as the whirlwind—

PIPES FROM PRAIRIE-LAND.

Smote as the arrow of heaven,
    The storm-flame, the lightning?—
"Mourns't thou the dead Wabishkizzi,
    Thy lover, the Pale-face?
Know the Great Spirit that slew him
    Was arrow of Chusco!"

On went the feast, the light dances,
    The songs and the stories.
Uprose Watooska, and calmly
    Made way through the rushes,
Passed the old wives and the maidens,
    Stood tall 'mid the chieftains—
Chanted: "Ningwegon, Megizze,
    O chieftains my fathers,
All ye bold Ottawa warriors,
    Ye braves of Ojibway,
Be peace sworn truly between you,
    And sealed by Watooska,
Sealed by the troth of White Lily
    To-day, unto Chusco,
Be that seal set now forever
    In smoke of the peace-pipe!"

Deftly she filled the deep pipe-bowl,
    And watched the weed kindle;

PIPES FROM PRAIRIE-LAND.

Followed with strained eyes, the curling
    Blue clouds of the peace-smoke;
Spoke yet again, her voice stealing
    Song-sweet on the silence:—
"One word give unto your daughter,
    I pray ye, my fathers.
Set is the seal with the peace-smoke—
    What power shall loose it?"
Reverent then, spake Ningwegon,
    "But One—the Great Spirit!"
Softly the Ottawas echoed,
    And all the Ojibways,
Chieftains, and rulers, and warriors,
    "But One—the Great Spirit!"

Over the face of Watooska
    Pale peace shone like moonlight.
Softly she cried to Megizze,
    "Bless, bless me, my father!"
Turned, as the old chief crooned fondly,
    "The Great Spirit bless thee!"
Swift as a deer, to the doorway;
    Sped out through the shadows,
Up to the rim of the forest,
    The crag crowned with pine trees.

PIPES FROM PRAIRIE-LAND.

What heard the guests as they followed,
    And crouched on the crag-brink?
Only the hiss of cut breezes
    Down, down the far fathoms—
Only the ringing, wild echoes,
    "I come, O my Pale-face!"

THE SHOOTING STAR.

"One of the most bewitching flowers in all the marvellous flora of Colorado."—H. H.

IN lonely canyon, in court of pines,
  Dwelt a kingly rock apart;
His crown of the virgin columbines,
  Yet sad in his great dark heart.

For night on night, in the sky above,
  There trembled a maiden star;
And the rock had looked his royal love,
  Yet she held her light afar.

He had donned white robes on winter night;
  He had trailed green gowns in June;
But the star still swung her vestal light,
  And laughed to the watching moon.

PIPES FROM PRAIRIE-LAND.

So lonely aye, in his court of pines,
    Dwelt the kingly rock apart,
His crown of the virgin columbines,
    Yet sad in his great dark heart.

Till one May night, in his sore despair,
    He ventured a ruse; and lo!
There lay on his breast, with blushing air,
    A rose from the vale below.

He held her close in his strong brown arms,
    And fondled her cheek's pink gloss;
And softly nestled her budding charms
    In a bed of velvet moss.

He dared the wound of her thorny sheath,
    And drank of her breast's sweet cup;
He drained deep, deep, of her fragrant breath,
    And then, he looked lightly up—

Looked lightly up to the sky above,
    Where trembled the maiden star
Who had seen him look his royal love,
    Yet had held her light afar.

PIPES FROM PRAIRIE-LAND.

They mingled one long, mute, midnight look—
  Then met in a burning kiss!
And clouds closed over an empty nook
  In the starry sky's abyss.

The hapless rose, o'er the pine's dark crest
  Was flung to the fields afar;
But pink and sweet on the rock's brown breast,
  Since, nestles a "shooting star."

THE RIVER ON THE PLAIN.

ON high Sierra a young spring glows,
White as a babe, from its natal snows.

The soft winds over its cradle sway;
Croon, as they rock it, a roundelay.

Their dewy chaplets tell mists in gray,
Veiling it chastely from day to day:

And flocks of raindrops, on earthward quest,
With light wings dimple its pulsing breast.

A crown of sunshine it dons, as born
Of ruddy Eos, the infant Morn:

A crown of starshine it dons by night,
Waiting the kiss of the pale moonlight:

As censors swaying, blown pines that guard,
Fan it with odors more sweet than nard,

PIPES FROM PRAIRIE-LAND.

And strong young eagles, on royal wing,
Winnow the heart of the mountain spring.

* * * *

Over the mountain a streamlet speeds,
Spurred by the prick of the bulrush reeds.

The woodbine tracks it from ledge to ledge,
Twining her tendrils along its edge:

A willowed army, with cedared flank,
Presses its pathway, close rank on rank:

And files of fir-trees, armèd with cones,
Riddle its picketing, lichened stones.

Bright bluffs and canyons it spans apace,
Clematis after, in purple chase:

Her wee green tassels the wild hop sways,
Listing its lyrics through sunny days:

The timid aspen takes heart and dips
Tremulous boughs for its warm young lips:

The blue wind-flower holds out her cup,
Yearning its ripples that sparkle up—

PIPES FROM PRAIRIE-LAND.

And coyly tinkles the plashed harebell,
Ringing the way to her citadel,

As down the mountain the streamlet speeds.
Spurred by the prick of the bulrush reeds.

* * * *

Over the prairie a river glides,
Tuft-grass a-tilt on its sloping sides.

Its white foam ripens to buds of spray,
Blooming the river as field of May:

It gaily sprinkles with opal show'r
Robes of the glittering mustard-flow'r:

Then slows and hushes, where rose on rose
Beside it anchors in pink repose.

Under the heavens, its clear tide glints
Rich as a rainbow in tangled tints:

And fair as Eden, along its flow,
Gardens of vetch in the sunlight glow.

Yet on forever, with panting breast,
Presses the river in vague unrest.

PIPES FROM PRAIRIE-LAND.

O, little recks it of mountain spring,
Winnowing eagles, and winds that sing!—

Of piney gulches it leaped in glee,
Chasing the blue-eyed anemone:

Of cloistered canyons with scented ways,
Flowery haunts of its early days.

For naught that has been, nor naught that is,
Merits the river's light loyalties—

But fairer ever, as moon than star,
Visions, that shadow what were or are,

Of goal that beckons, whose fair shores lie
On the veiled breast of futurity.

Alas! O river, not we, not we,
Meetly may chide of disloyalty!

Nor bid you tarry, while yet you may,
Prizing the bloom of your sunny way—

For we, too, reckon to-day a bond,
And yearn the morrow that waits beyond.

PIPES FROM PRAIRIE-LAND.

What is, is nothing; what shall be, all.
So runs it ever, and ever shall—

Till as a river that meets the sea,
Finiteness ripes to Infinity!

A PRAIRIE FLOWER.

ONCE on the prairie red with June,
 (O, for the sweet June hour!)
Fond skies sending to her baptism
Warm winds for sponsors, and dews for chrism,
 Blossomed a human flower.

Set in the waste of prairie grass
 Like star in an empty heaven,
Out from an aureole of hair
Her virgin face, with the haloed air
 Of young May moon at even.

Blue as the gentian-bells her eyes;
 Fresh as the winds that hover
Soft on the high Sierra peaks,
The fitful bloom of her wildrose cheeks,
 Dimpled their pink hearts over.

Cradled in suns and snows she rocked
 Out of her young bud, lithely;

PIPES FROM PRAIRIE-LAND.

Out of her bud, (as birdlings wing
Swift way from the nest's safe sheltering,)
  Into her fair bloom, blithely.

Came Love then, with a lilt and lay—
  Love that is light and airy;
Wove a snare of a golden thread,
Tangled her heart in its mesh and sped
  Out from the red June prairie:

Bore her swiftly and bore her far—
  (Ah, for the sad June hour!)
Now in jewels and robes of state,
With wistful eyes, at the city gate,
  A pale young prairie flower.

JUANITA.

OUT, like a star from the midnight,
    Flashes her face, from the splendid
      Warm depths of her hair:
Under arched brows, olive-lidded,
Eyes pensive and passioned; woman
      With child adream there.

Royal dark cheeks, faintly oval;
Daintily dimpled, and glowing
      With youth bright as sun:
Lips rarely proud, withal tender;
Crescent-curved; smiles sweet as roses
      In blushes thereon.

Throat arching softly to shoulder:
Arms for caressing; slight-wristed;
      Slim hands brown and firm:
Young breast athrob with unconscious,
Shy dreams, whence years shall discover
      Love warm in the germ.

PIPES FROM PRAIRIE-LAND.

Supple, round limbs, clearly veinèd,
Lithe as spring boughs; swift and stealthy
    To flee or to track:
Flaming their basilisk beauty,
Savage blood traced to red chieftains
    Proud centuries back.

Nay, veil that glance—she is holy!
Round her young days, as a halo,
    The blight of her race.
Wild and unrestful her spirit
Under the glow of her bosom,
    The flash of her face.

Exile of trackless pine forests,
Exile of natal brown wigwam,
    She wanders apart,
Holding the hates of her fathers;
Beating like bird on her fetters
    With passionate heart.—

Brown maid Juanita, one balm is,
Potent to soothe thy sore spirit,
    As near years shall prove.
Sweeter than scent of thy pine-trees,
Warmer than teepe or wigwam,
    Juanita, is—love!

A WESTERN WEDDING.

O GOLDEN blows the summer wind! The summer rose blooms red—
The little birds are singing sweet in branches overhead,
And softly down the meadow-path the clover-scent is shed.

The clover down the meadow-path, blent with the fragrant pine;
Pale yuccas by the roadside wave, and ruddy vetches twine;
And round the farmhouse, daisies drift, and bright tuft-grasses shine.

Sweet honeysuckle climbs the warm, brown rafters to the vane;
Grapevines above the threshold hang their tangled summer chain,
And roses up the casement-sills, tap at each open pane.

PIPES FROM PRAIRIE-LAND.

The great barn nestles close behind, corn stacked beside, in rows;
Within, birds twitter from the beams, and hens on soft nests drowse;
The new hay shimmers in the loft; in bins the ripe grain glows.

Ungathered in west orchards hang round apples on the trees;
No step the languid meadows wakes, adream in the south breeze;
The grainfields waver north and east, like lone, unridden seas.

No sickle sweeps, nor groan the wains; freed horses graze at will;
Unyokèd oxen slowly stray in wake of the swift rill;
The milch-cows, unmolested doze in shadow of the hill.

For chores are done, and fieldwork left, and daily stints put by;
The neighbors to the farmhouse flock from hearthstones far and nigh,
And of a bridal sing the birds unto the summer sky.

PIPES FROM PRAIRIE-LAND.

O, but a maiden is the bride, maid-sweet, and fresh and fair!
The good old priest a blessing prays as she trips down the stair,
Upon her cheek the red, red rose, the gold wind in her hair.

The red, red rose upon her cheek, the white rose on her breast;
Soft tears within her frank brown eyes, that happy smiles contest,
And shy lips tunèd to the vows of sanctioned love, and bless'd.

The farmfolk mutely gather round; the merry guests are still;
The honeysuckle joins the rose, and tarries on the sill;
And singing birds their carols hush, to list her low "I will."

The glad young lover links the ring, and seals it with a kiss;
And when the gay folk follow suit, takes it no whit amiss,
Till shyly seeks the bride his side, and prays an armistice.

Then leads the cordial housewife out, where waits the bridal-board;
A smile is on her face, but ah! within her heart a sword,
For from her harp of life to-day, is rent the golden chord.

PIPES FROM PRAIRIE-LAND.

With creamèd coffee brim the cups; the sweet young cider flows;
Red jellies glow like wine between curds white as drifted snows;
The frost upon the bridal-cake is crowned by one white rose.

The toasts are drunk; the speeches done; the flute and viol play;
The young folk start a merry dance; the bride steals soft away,
And up the stair she flits in white, and down the stair in gray.

Still on her breast the white, white rose; still on her cheek, the red;
She smiles but faintly, and her eyes are deep with tears unshed,
For love has crossed her woof of life, and snapped the virgin thread.

She is all faith, she is all fear; all sorrow and all bliss;
She is so new to life and love, what if she prove remiss?
She trembles as her sweet lips seek the parting parent-kiss.

PIPES FROM PRAIRIE-LAND.

The proud groom takes her little hand, and lays it on his arm;
She steals a glance at his glad face, and chides her vague alarm;
She strives to smile, and smiling turns her face from the old farm.

The white rice patters on her path; the lucky shoe falls near;
She waves a kiss back to the folk, who answer with a cheer;
But on the grasses, as she stands, there shines a fallen tear.

Across the fields a white house gleams, the sun upon its dome;
A gilded vane looks from the roof, and beckons her to come.
The happy bridegroom bends his head, and softly whispers "Home!"

His lips are warm; his eyes are glad; his heart beats high with pride;
He leads her up the flowered lane, and sets the bars aside,
And on the threshold, ere they cross, he kisses his young bride.

AN AUTUMN CANTER.

WIDE and windy the skies hang over,
    Linked clouds riding their dizzy height;
On to the prairie speeds the plover,
    Cut winds hissing along her flight.

Brown Fall woods shed a leafy shower,
    Brown Fall grasses drift down the plain;
Shades of night to the mountain lower,
    Hung on silver, slant ropes of rain.

Great firs filing the rocky passes,
    Crisp shot volley in russet cones;
Gray mists coiling in smoky masses
    Over the riddled mountain stones.

On, my charger! the far mists guide us;
    Lashed skies press on our speeding way;
Gold leaves race with the red, beside us;—
    On, through the royal, rare Fall day!

PIPES FROM PRAIRIE-LAND.

What if the heavens dark and glower?
   What if the threatened rain fall fast?
Sweeter than sun the fresh Fall shower;
   Sweeter than song, the ringing blast.

O, to fetter this perfect hour
   Fast as fate, to thy glancing reins!
O, to hold for a lasting dower,
   New life flaming my kindled veins!

O, to ride to the Red Man's heaven!
   O, that the Hunting Grounds were near!
O, to shoe thee with Jovic leven,
   Spurring thee onward, year by year,

Up the height of the sun's gold gateway,
   Up the sky, through the moon's warm bars;
Up to the winds, to race them straightway
   Swift abreast, through the watching stars!

Borne on wing of thy strong, fleet motion,
   Deep and deeper, in god-like bliss,
Rare a nectar as great Jove's potion
   Quaff my lips in the wind's fierce kiss.

Who that tastes of a god's libation
   Will not drain, though the lees be death?

PIPES FROM PRAIRIE-LAND.

Back not I, to the old stagnation,
   Slow, calm pulses, and even breath!

On, nor falter! On so, forever,
   Brave my bearer, with hoofs of speed!
All behind do I gladly sever—
   On forever, O gallant steed!

MOWING THE HARVEST HAY.

THE late sun furls her golden sails,
    And turns her red prow west;
The wind blows sweet with rye and wheat,
    The bluejay seeks her nest.
The patient kine wind to the ranch,
    The homeward horses neigh;
And down the grass the swift scythes pass,
    Mowing the harvest hay.

The brown young farmer walks beside,
    And cheers the meek team on;
His eyes are blue, his heart is true,
    And warm as summer sun.
He gaily whistles tune on tune,
    To while the time away,
As down the grass the swift scythes pass,
    Mowing the harvest hay.

From the near barn a clear voice calls
    The milch-cows one by one;

PIPES FROM PRAIRIE-LAND.

Beside the gates the farmer waits—
  The faithful team goes on.
The pretty milkmaid leaves her pails,
  To hear what he would say,
And down the grass the scythes still pass,
  Mowing the harvest hay.

O sweet old tale that never tires!
  O love forever new!—
The dusk to hear, steals softly near,
  Adown her bridge of dew.
The brown young farmer pleads his prayer,
  The pretty maid says "Aye"—
And down the grass the swift scythes pass,
  Mowing the harvest hay.

ATTUNED.

DOWN the dim mountains drifts the gloam;
    The nightwinds wake and sigh;
Deep shadows hang the lurid dome
    Of storm-horizoned sky.

Monks of the lone Sierra crests,
    Mute pines, in mournful row,
Their vigils keep, with barèd breasts
    Long disciplined with snow.

From their high springs slant streamlets sail
    With ghostly prows of foam,
And masts of mist, that unfurl pale
    Wet sheets along the gloam.

On the dank bloom dews glimmer chill
    As tears in faded eyes;
Across the hush, aloft and shrill,
    A stray cayote cries.

PIPES FROM PRAIRIE-LAND.

No sunbeam lingers from the day:
    No star breaks out apace;
Upon the plain the dusk lies gray
    As death on human face—

And like mute heart whose chords of pain
    Vibrate 'neath some soft hand,
Swept by the wind, the dumb clouds rain
    Wet notes along the land.

No village orbed with twinkling light,
    In the lone distance lies;
No cottage lamp sheds on the night
    The glow the moon denies.

All, all is dark and chill and lone,
    From doming sky, to nave
Of wild grass tangled round the stone
    That marks a lonely grave.

THE HUSKING OF THE CORN.

THE sweet hay scales the rafters,
    The oats are in the bin;
The harvests are all garnered,
    The fruit is gathered in.
The cider foams the tankard,
    The farmer sounds the horn,
And bids us to the husking,
    The husking of the corn.

      O the husking of the corn,
        The husking of the corn!
      And O, to find the red ear,
        The shy red ear of corn!—
      To tear the husks asunder,
        And when the cob is shorn,
      To kiss the girl I love, at
        The husking of the corn.

Within the cheery farmhouse
    The ruddy pine-logs glow;

PIPES FROM PRAIRIE-LAND.

The lamps flame at the casements,
   And light the fields below;
While in the barn adjoining,
   That shining stacks adorn,
We gather for the husking,
   The husking of the corn.

     O the husking of the corn, etc., etc.

The crisp sheaves rive and rustle,
   The silk twines into curls;
The shorn cobs glimmer chastely
   In vestal veils of pearls;
And when from rosy kernels
   The clinging husks are torn,
O merry grows the husking,
   The husking of the corn!

     O the husking of the corn, etc., etc.

The stacks sink low and lower,
   The huskèd ears are stored;
Within the bright farm-kitchen
   We throng the festal board.
And o'er the sparkling cider,
   Ah! who has heart to scorn

PIPES FROM PRAIRIE-LAND.

The merry, merry husking,
  The husking of the corn!

    O the husking of the corn, etc., etc.

And when the feast is over,
  To crown the husker's weal,
The fiddler seeks the hearthstone,
  And shyly sounds the reel;
Then trips each lad and lassie
  The happy dance till morn,
All at the merry husking,
  The husking of the corn.

    O the husking of the corn, etc., etc.

Then O, the noisy going,
  The tying on of hoods,
The ride across the prairie,
  Or through the dark pine woods!
And ah! the soft words spoken,
  And ah! the sweet faiths sworn,
All going from the husking,
  The husking of the corn!

    O the husking of the corn,
      The husking of the corn!

PIPES FROM PRAIRIE-LAND.

 And O, to find the red ear
  The shy red ear of corn!
 To tear the husks asunder,
  And when the cob is shorn,
 To kiss the girl I love, at
  The husking of the corn.

THE DESERTED CABIN.

SIERRAS.

THE lone gulch shrouds it wierdly
    In snows untrod and deep;
To pines behind, the winter wind
    Sobs from drear steep to steep.

No sun it knows, nor starlight,
    Nor glow of northern lights;
For grim between, the mountains lean,
    With glaciers up their heights.

The three-month snows are drifted
    Within the unhinged door;
And gleam in white, through day and night,
    On the untrodden floor.

The casement creaks, and clashes
    Its dangling swords of ice,
Unsheathed and bare, and wrought in rare,
    Chill shapes of quaint device.

PIPES FROM PRAIRIE-LAND.

Down from the riven rafters,
  And hoary walls of pine,
Keen scimitars for mimic wars
  Glint in a frosty line.

While from one lonely corner,
  With snowflakes for a crown,
Nailed to the Tree of Calvary,
  A silver Christ looks down.

    *   *   *   *

O fond and faithful spirit
  This cross does mutely tell!
What fate may stay thine absent way,
  Ill farest thou, or well?

The chill snows drift in palely;
  The pine trees sob and sway;
The fierce winds shriek from peak to peak:
  Their answer—who shall say?

A SORGHUM CANDY-PULL.

FIVE miles out from house or village stands the old farm on the prairie;
From its roof red lanterns dangle, lest we miss the lonely way.
Lamps are shining at each window, in the barn and in the dairy,
And red pine-flames on the snowdrifts o'er the kitchen threshold play.
Rows of sleighs stand in the barnyard; rows of steeds paw in the stable;
There is sound of many voices, then a sudden listing lull,
As we sweep through the great gateway to the porch beneath the gable,
Where the farmer bids us welcome to the sorghum candy-pull.

At the door his good wife curtsies, with both hands outstretched in greeting;
Points us up to the front chamber, where young voices bid us "Come!"

PIPES FROM PRAIRIE-LAND.

And we file up the wide stairway, followed still by her entreating
That we "Give th' gals our bunnits, an' jest make ourselves t' hum."
On the top stair wait her daughters, twin wild-roses blushing newly
In their fear lest "city-people find wild weste'n doin's dull"—
Till their warm young hands enfolding, we assure them, (and most truly,)
That we know no sweeter frolic than a sorghum candy-pull.

As we enter the bright kitchen, the gray host presents us duly:—
"Friends, th' city-folks from east'ards, ez is stoppin' ter Mis' Est's."
And the bows and handshakes over, the red logs are kindled newly,
And a hush of expectation deepens 'mong the waiting guests.
Then from off the high pine dresser comes the great, brass shining kettle,
And the farm-wife pours the sorghum till the girls proclaim it full;

PIPES FROM PRAIRIE-LAND.

When they lift it to the fire, and the farmer from his settle,
Claps his knee, and hurrahs gaily for the sorghum candy-pull.

As the pine-flames leap and crackle, we can see the sorghum stealing
In great golden coils that shimmer round the kettle's circled brim;
And the lads crowd to the pantry, tall heads dodging the low ceiling,
For the great spoons peeping brightly from the shelf's rosetted rim.
Then what gallantry and blushes, as each to his chosen maiden
Holds the shining pewter handle, the deep bowl still in his hand;
And the pretty, quaint procession, as they file in twains, so laden,
And group gaily round the kettle, at the leader's blithe command!

Swift the first spoon seeks the sorghum, and the stirring goes on fleetly,
Two hands clasped about the handle, hers for holding, his to guide;

PIPES FROM PRAIRIE-LAND.

And as o'er the ruddy hearthstone, soft young cheeks flush
out so sweetly,
O, I dream the flames steal deeper, and warm soft young
hearts, beside!
And as twain each twain replaces, till the spoons have all
been christened,
Sitting back in the still corner, while the kettle brims and
boils,
To my heart float faint, stray echoes of shy words the
fire has listened,
As the spoons went slowly circling through the golden
sorghum-coils.

Out unto the ice-bound bucket go the last twain, snows
unheeding,
For a bowl of water sparkling from the well, like rare old
wine;
And what pretty, anxious faces, and what rapture swift
succeeding,
As the sorghum seeks the bottom in a crisp and brittle
line!
Then the putting out of platters; routing of canine
infringers;
And the restless time of waiting till the frosty air shall
cool;

PIPES FROM PRAIRIE-LAND.

And the eager choice of partners, and the buttering of fingers,
As the farm-wife names the candy as all ready for the pull.

What a merry tussle follows, with the golden ropes that shimmer
Titian-red between the embers, and the lamps of ruddy light;
And what rival boasts and daring, while the gold grows ever dimmer,
Till the yellow merges slowly first to cream and then to white!
What an awed and anxious silence, as from defter hands fall gleaming
Hearts, and rings, and blent initials, linkèd in true lovers' knots—
And what calls for water, after, for the sticky palms' redeeming,
And what girlish toss of ribands, and what brushing off of spots!

Then the bearing of the candy, in a great dish to the table
In the dining-room adjoining, where the juicy apples wait;

PIPES FROM PRAIRIE-LAND.

Where the giant-jugs of cider foam like nectar of old fable,
And the nuts for philopening lie in lone and dusky state.
And the merry hours that follow, winged in jest and song and laughter,
While the apples grow but phantoms, and the nuts but shells that seem,
And the cider ebbs out surely as the candy, that leaves after
But the lovers' knots, that cherished, pledge each maid a charmèd dream.

Twelve strokes echo from the stairway, ere the last good-nights are spoken,
Ere the steeds turn from the stables, and the sleighs stand at the door;
And the farmfolk from the threshold, after each, in kindly token,
Throw a pippin from the basket newly filled from their rich store.
As the merry sleighs speed by us, I lean back against the cushion,
And the moonlight blinds me strangely, for my eyes and heart are full,
As I question if my city, with its eastern wealth and fashion,
Boasts so truly sweet a frolic as a sorghum candy-pull.

IN THE ORIGINAL KEY.

"YE whose hearts are fresh and simple,
       Who have faith in God and Nature,
Who believe that in all ages
Every human heart is human,
That in even savage bosoms
There are longings, yearnings, strivings,
For the good they comprehend not,
That the feeble hands and helpless,
Groping blindly in the darkness,
Touch God's right hand in that darkness
And are lifted up and strengthened;
Listen to these simple stories,
To these songs of mine and meadow."

    Adapted from LONGFELLOW'S "HIAWATHA."

A PIONEER POET.

SEE thet tent thar, whar' th' grass
    Follers up th' mounting-pass?
See thet chap ez looks a clown,
Walkin' slowly up an' down?
Thar's his tent, sir, an' thar's him
Ez ye axed fur—poet Jim.

Wot on 'arth folks gits ter see
In thet feller, squelches me.
Dashed ef I hain't showed th' way
Three more times afore, terday.
Nuthin' much, he ain't, in looks—
S'pose ye've hearn ez he writes books?
'Read em?' Jest draw mild, pard! Me?—
Ya—as! thet's jest th' sort I be.

Knowed his father; me an' him
Onct wuz pards. He wuz a limb,
Old Jim wuz in his young days,
Till one year he tuk a craze

IN THE ORIGINAL KEY.

Fur a gal ez with her par
Kem ter summer on th' Bar.—
W'ite an' peaky; a poor lot—
Not my style by a long shot!
Full o' flowery, high talk
Ez hed nary stem nor stalk.
Howsomever, Jim wuz struck
Hard an' hot; an' she, wuss luck,
Caved-in ter his han'some face,
Settled down in thet same place;
Stayin' jest till thet chap kum,
Then put out her light, sir, plum'!
Jim died later, fifteen year,
Jest ez he hed struck luck here—
Left his claim an' tent ter him,
Thet poor chap thar—poet Jim.

W'u'dn't guess it, seein' him,
But he hed th' sass, hed Jim,
Ter git sweet upon my gal—
My one darter, sir, my Sal.
Hi! but thet night D's wuz thick—
I swar some, I did, by Nick!
Sal, she cried, ez wimmen do,
But I guess she'll live it thro'.

IN THE ORIGINAL KEY.

'Taint fur her, so peart an' trim,
Ter be jest Mis' Poet Jim!

Hain't no gumption, thet Jim hain't—.
Gosh! his ways 'ud rile a saint.
Works a spell, when he's cleaned out,
Then jest idles roun' about,
Roamin' up an' down th' pass,
Lyin' in th' summer grass,
Starin' up them same old skies,
(Ez is kin ter his blue eyes—)
Watchin' now, jest a wild rose
Bowin' ez th' breezes blows,
Lookin' up et them dark pines
Yaller when th' noon sun shines,
Countin' all th' birds thet fly,
Smilin', sighin'; by an' by
Sets ter writin' fur dear life—
Nice chap thet, ter hev' a wife!

Wot's his line—trees, birds, an' stars,
Ain't it? Tho't so! Like his mar's.
'Fore she merried, she writ, too,
Hevin' nuthin' more ter do.
Gals afore they git a beau
Kinder find life dull, ye know,

IN THE ORIGINAL KEY.

An' some high uns tek ter rhyme,
Jest ter pass away th' time—
W'ich I ain't on leanin' rough,
Ez they'll drop it sharp enough
Et a chance ter settle down,
With a man an' babies roun'.
But a chap with no more vim
Then ter be a poet, like Jim—
Shunt it, pard, it makes me sick!—
Eh? O thankee! Yer a brick!

Some like—thet! More? No, pard, no!—
Wal, I don't keer—let her go!
Ain't no poet, ye ain't, sir! Hey?
Blast my ears, wot's thet ye say?
Jest thet same, sir? Wal, I vum!
Dern my boots ef thet ain't rum!
Tuk ye fur a tearin' swell.—
Jest a poet? Ain't thet a sell!

Eh? Good Lord! Let me set down!
Jim th' talk o' town on town?
Great folks thro' th' hull wide land
Holdin' him warm heart an' hand?
Him th' pride o' comin' times,
Jest thro' his falutin' rhymes?

IN THE ORIGINAL KEY.

Him a gen'us—him a star—
His name ringin' near an' far—
Gold a-runnin' up his claim?
Gosh!—
    O Jim, I say! Jest aim
Roun' our way some night, an'—wal,
S'pose ye jest talk over Sal?

DARE-DEVIL DICK.

SO! the play's at an end,
   And the curtain rung down
And the hero, old friend,
   Makes his bow to the town
   With cold death for a crown.

Where both laurel and bay
   Once entwined me, I vow—
Where love's red roses lay
   Warm as kiss on my brow,
   Creeps the chill cypress, now.

Thirty years, to a day,
   Since Dame Fate threw the bone
Labelled Life, in my way;
   And I, poor dog, disown
   That bone now, as a stone!

IN THE ORIGINAL KEY.

What is living, but pain?
    What is hope, but a cheat?
What is love, but a vein
    That with hot ebb, and sweet,
    Falters out at Time's feet?—

Full my cup to the brim
    With life's wine, and I laugh'd
O'er the glowing, red rim,
    And drank deep, till I quaff'd
    The death-lees of the draught.

O my golden, proud youth,
    And the plaudits mine then,
When I reigned in all truth
    From the throne of my pen,
    As a prince among men!—

O ye reckless, wild days,
    When I served at the shrine
Of two gods fit for praise—
    Love and Bacchus! Divine
    Days of women and wine!—

O ye after-days here
    In this rogue's paradise,

IN THE ORIGINAL KEY.

Where I end my career
   To the chink of wined ice,
   And the ring of the dice!—

Have ye led but to this?
   Do ye hold but this goal—
Red with Lorette's last kiss,
   Red with lees of the bowl,
   Death, death, body and soul?

Ah, that blood! D—— it! Pass
   That red wine there. God! Quick!
Say: He drank his last glass
   To the health of old Nick—
   Did bold dare-devil Dick!

A BORDER ROMANCE.

A YARN? Lemme see! Wot's yer style? Poetry, hey?
   Well, I reckon thet ain't my line.
This border-life 'yer I hain't allers found play,
   Nor struck much o' poetry in mine.

Yet things sometimes comes ter us boys, ez sounds well
   When a poet-chap hauls out his rhyme,
An' mebbe—'yer, jest ye set down fur a spell,
   An' give this 'yer slow feller time.

Glad ye happened along. Them theer's on a spree,
   So I shunted off from their den,
An' lit my pipe 'yer, a streak bein' in me
   Ez likes solitood now an' then;

An' often o' evenin's, I shake off th' lot,
   An' smokin' 'yer, under th' sky,
Sorter start my thoughts off on a backward trot
   Ter th' days ez is long went by.

IN THE ORIGINAL KEY.

Sho, now! Jest quit pokin' yer fun ter my nose!
    Me a poet? Well, jokin' apart,
Thar's mebbe more poetry 'n most folks suppose,
    Hid deep in a rough feller's heart!

Which mine, sech ez 'tiz, sence ye think it wuth while,
    Ye're welcome to, pard, so 'yer goes;
An' ef ye don't find it jest arter yer style,
    Ye might mebbe tack it ter prose.—

Thet moon, like a pale woman-face in th' sky,
    Th' wind moanin' sad thro' th' pines,
An' them shadders driftin' like waves slowly by,
    Down th' shafts o' th' lonely mines,

Some'ow brings ter my mind a night I onct seen
    A-minin' up yon, on th' Bar—
A blade from th' coast, ez wuz yet in th' green,
    But counted ter be on th' squar'.

Well, lyin' alone in my tent this 'yer night,
    An' pinin', not hevin' no pard,
Th' boys an' me not hitchin' well ez we might,
    Me not playin' nor drinkin' hard—

A shadder kem quick-like, twixt me an' th' light
    O' th' moon, like thet thar un, dim;

IN THE ORIGINAL KEY.

An' th' frightened, pale face o' a lad kem in sight,
    Th' boys, like mad hounds, arter him.

A poor un, thet lad, fur a lad; small an' lean,
    With a voice ez soft ez a bird's;
Weak et work ez a gal; an' skeery an' green
    Ez I couldn't put inter words.

No day more'n eighteen, an' a poor un fur thet,
    With a young face smooth ez a pear;
Big eyes like thet heart's-ease thar, purple an' wet,
    An' a roofin' o' yaller hair.

Th' boys meant no harm, bein' jest on a spree
    Fur th' night, an' not bad et heart,
But rough ez a crowd, fur thet lad, an' burn me!
    I jest couldn't but tek his part.

So up went th' flap o' my tent, ez he pass'd,
    An' in he wuz pulled, sharp ez shot;
He pantin' fur breath like a roe et her last,
    Ez I waited ter face th' lot.

They kem in a pack, with their teeth set fur game,
    An' th' lad got shaky an' white,
But onct rile my blood, an' I'm all sot aflame—
    An' I wuzn't put back one mite,

IN THE ORIGINAL KEY.

Fur this six-shooter 'yer, wuz safe in one hand,
    An' safe in th' t'other, its mate;
An' I kinder suspicioned they'd tek a stand
    Ez them sharps didn't kalkerlate.

So I up with my hands, an' quiet an' slow,
    Sez: "Kum, boys, ter one o' yer size."
An' barks o' them dogs o' a suddin wuz low,
    In a sickly sort o' surprise.

Sez I: "I ain't much on hard drink, ez ye know,
    Nor keerds, so I ain't half a man,
But jest thet fur growed thet I like blow fur blow,
    Which ain't jest th' size o' yer plan.

"Jest thet near a man, thet I like fightin' fa'r,
    An' hit whar thar's some hittin' back;
An' yer fully-growed sharps 'll be derned more squar'
    When they tumble on thet same tack.—

"Which I've only ter say thet from this night on,
    This lad he'll be under my keer,
An' all jokers is welcome ter tek their fun
    Out o' me, an' my pardners 'yer!"

Which th' moon, ez wuz low, shun out like a brick,
    An' these poppers, they showed out fine;

IN THE ORIGINAL KEY.

An' them cowards, they kinder got pale an' sick,
    An' turned tail in a sharp B line.

An' from thet night ter this, thet poor lad an' me,
    We've be'n pards ez is pards fur life.—
Don't guess? Sho! Look thar by my tent. Don't ye see?
    Thar's th' lad—thet woman—my wife!

AT THE MOUTH OF THE TUNNEL.

WOT are you starin' at? Can't a girl cry,
   But you must be knowin' the how an' why?
A poet, now, ain't you? I know your style.
Down close by the fiddles, front chair, left aisle,
You figgered last evenin', an' when I died,
You clapped me—an' snickered in stage aside.
Well, mebbe my actin' ain't Bern'art's yet,
But there's that more tragic you'd like, I bet,
(You bein' a poet, an' up to time
Fur points as 'll posture up well, in rhyme—)
I can tell you, deadhead, of an affair
Twixt me, an' him—dead—in the tunnel there.

I'd brazened the footlights, an' gone about
Fur two or more seasons, to towns set out,
When last March, at twilight, we somehow struck
On this here Black Tunnel, in stroke of luck.
I've taken well allers, play wot I might,
But that time—" M'liss " headed the bills that night,

IN THE ORIGINAL KEY.

An' I played it splendid, with all my art,
An' with wot's more tellin', my woman's heart—)
Along with my takin' this here hull town,
I was taken myself, which warn't writ down,
By a big chap fillin' a chair to right—
Joe Smith, as they're diggin fur, here, to-night!

We'd a run that Sunday across a streak
Of the lone March prairie, brown, bare, and bleak.
The sad winds was sobbin', an' blew the rain
Like great tears a-splashin' my window-pane.
I must hev' been nerv'us, I guess, an' low,
As us poor weak wimmin will be, you know,
Fur it seemed them raindrops jest wept fur me—
(I *must* hev' been nerv'us an' low, you see.)
Fur the life, good, blameless, I might hev' led,
With a godlier heart, an' wiser head;
An' I gev' up hopin' to walk more straight,
Fur them winds kept sobbin', "Too late! too late!"

I ain't jest ill-favored, as you may see,
Nor saint more 'n others as lives like me;
An' the fun that's offered, I've up an' had,
With no "nice distinctions" twixt good an' bad.
Which that same, sir, knowin', an' owned to-night,
Is a truth but seldom so clear in sight;

IN THE ORIGINAL KEY.

Fur I've allers argu'd, when sore at heart,
As how some was casted fur soubrette-part
In Life, that's God's drama, sir, arter all—
An' it ain't too often that I, here, fall
In a mood so sober as on that day,
That no overture-chords could play away.

Well, the curtain lifted; I got my cue,
An' the boards was taken with dash, tell you!
Fur I'd jest swore mildly, in makin' up,
That I'd not miss, leastways, the winning cup
On the only race-track left sech as me,
An' it ain't hard guessin' which that one be.
An' lookin' out over the row of lights—
The stars as us actors loves best o' nights—
Two eyes, blue an' gentle, looked inter mine,
An' I felt as justly I can't define,
But so as we only feel onct on earth,
When love trembles, babe-like, in pangs of birth.

That strong I was taken, there seemed none there
But jest him, sir, han'some, with wavy hair.—
Sech a big, grave feller, as looked all true,
An' I played so pointed he caught the cue.
The house, it was crowded; the boys they cheered;
But he jest set quiet till all was cleared,

IN THE ORIGINAL KEY.

An' then, of a sudden, he took the wings,
An' caught me still flauntin' in last-act things,
With my face all painted, an' pencilled eyes,
An' wot does I do, sir, in sharp surprise,
But mindless of powder an' toggery,
Jest add to the program, a woman's cry!

You see, I hed fancied my life laid bare
In his eyes' blue mirrors, as he set there;
An' I seen me plainly, as I jest be,
Not bad at the bottom, but bold an' free,
An' brushin' too nearly the shame of life,
To ever be counted a good man's wife.
An' the day seemed over to turn or mend,
An' my heart seen nary an other end
Then jest to go on'ards from bad to worse,
To the last-night exit, in a black hearse;
So I cried an' cried, sir, an' thro' my tears,
Sobbed out all the feelin's I'd crushed fur years.

"He said—?" Beg your pardon, but jest that, I
Can't quite tell, or leastways, I shan't; an' why
Won't be all a riddle, if you've yet be'n
In that line of drama us two struck then.
True love is a greenroom, shut to the crowd!
An' first sight, Joe loved me—a point allowed

IN THE ORIGINAL KEY.

As not out of natur, where much is chance,
By me, who am livin' by stage-romance,
An' you, as a poet, with seein' eyes
Fur things as don't allers go commonwise.
An' purer or truer, no love could be
Than fate billed fur *début* that night, fur me.

Things comes to us people in crooked lines,
In ways as don't trouble the Philistines;
An' mebbe a woman not on the stage,
Nor deep inter poetry, (the latest rage—)
Wouldn't jest hev' fallen in love that way,
But I ain't shamefaced, sir, to up an' say
As that dear chap held me, from that first night,
By a chain I cherished with main an' might.
An' shiftin' our scenics, I gev' my vow,
(Which he ain't, poor feller, fur claimin', now!)
That nuthin' should hold me, when his call came,
From new boards took under his honest name.

I think we'd hev' married, sir, there an' then,
But luck wasn't friendly as might hev' be'n;
He was poor an' haughty as chap might be,
An' wouldn't take kindly to wot struck me—
That we might be married, an' me still play;
So our ways they parted, one gray March day,

IN THE ORIGINAL KEY.

An' sence, we've be'n doin' our common best
To lay somethin' by, sir. You know the rest.
We'd jest sighted clearly our daily bread,
An' my "Last Appearance" the posters read
Last night.—The play's over.—To-night was billed
Fur us two to marry, an'—Joe—is—killed!

Seems hard, kinder, don't it? An' yet I know
Jest why this here climax was worked up so.—
His heart, it was pure, sir, an' mine was black,
An' the two warn't never fur single track.
My best I meant surely; but p'raps 'twas writ,
An' me an' him never aguessin' it—
That as time went on'ards, an' me his wife,
I might jest grow restless fur the old life,
An' take a step back'ards, or strike out wrong,
In some line of badness, with him along;
An' so, this here cave-in was meant to be,
To save the poor feller, jest, sir, from me!

Wot's that? O, I'll stop here till he's laid out,
Then strike, bag and baggage, fur the old route—
Be blazed on the posters, pose as a star,
Flirt over the footlights, etcetera.
Jest turn out the moral fur good or worse,
An' ring down the curtain as best in verse—

IN THE ORIGINAL KEY.

But the truth, (if called fur,) is that I'll make
A "special" of virtue, fur his dear sake.
The rôle is a new one, an' not my line,
But please God! in Joe's name, I'll make it mine,
An' then—don't you think, sir, a day *may* be
When we won't be parted—my Joe an' me?

WHILE THE WHITE CORN POPS.

DRAW the heavy curtains closer—
   We will shut out the wild night.
Pile the pine-logs high and higher;
   Trim anew the crimson light.
Bring the settle to the hearthstone,
   Where the ruddy pine-flames glow :—
Naught care we for winter weather,
   Bitter night, or cold white snow.
From the cellar bear the apples,
   And the brown nuts stored beside;
Tap the cider till it gushes
   In a foamy, golden tide;
Fill the quaint old glasses waiting,
   To their shining, crystal tops—
And be
    Merry,
       Merry,
          Merry,
While the white corn pops!

IN THE ORIGINAL KEY.

Steal the book away from father,
  Set the mother's knitting by;
Let us all be young together
  While we watch the kernels fly.
Gold or crimson, which is riper?—
  (Bring the great dish from the shelf.—)
Hear the fierce wind down the chimney,
  Like a hungry, thievish elf!
(Get the salt from out the pantry—
  Fill the popper once again.)
Hear the little snow-hands tapping
  On the shutters and the pane!
Ah! what wonder they would enter?
  For the frolic never stops,
But is
    Merry,
        Merry,
            Merry,
While the white corn pops.

(Stir the popped corn in the sorghum
  If you want a bar or ball.)—
Shall I tell you a true story?
  Listen well, now, one and all!
Once a little farmhouse lifted
  From a prairie lone and wide;

IN THE ORIGINAL KEY.

Once a sweet lass sat within it,
   A rough fellow by her side,
Who had loved her warm and truly,
   Many a long day and night,
But to tell her he strove vainly,
   For she always took to flight.—
(What, Ruth, going? Nay, girl, never!
   Hear my story till it stops,
And be
     Merry,
        Merry,
           Merry,
   While the white corn pops.)

Well, he waited long and vainly,
   But the lassie still was coy,
Till at last her lover thought him
   Of a ruse he might employ.
So as snows fell white and fleetly,
   On the winds of winter borne,
What did he but ask—"Her answer?"
   Nay—the popper and the corn!
And a seat she scarce had taken
   At his plain-expressed desire,
Close beside him on the settle
   Drawn before the bright pine-fire,

IN THE ORIGINAL KEY.

When he pleaded:—(Ruth, dear, listen!)
  "Ere the summer ripes the crops,
Will you
        Marry,
                Marry?
                      Tell me,
  While the white corn pops!"

What the lassie said, I know not.
  Ruth here, maybe, knows the rest.
Bid her speak, O father, mother,
  Who my little ruse have guess'd!
And your pity I claim surely,
  For a lover so forlorn,
He can pop the question only
  While a-popping of the corn.
Now, Ruth, put away your blushes,
  And say clearly, yes or no!
"Yes?" O father, lay the book down—
  Mother, let the knitting go!
Let us all be young together,
  Now the clock of time, love stops—
And be
        Merry,
                Merry,
                      Merry,
  While the white corn pops.

AN OPEN LETTER.

THE moon, like a gold ship, is sailing the sky,
  With tiny star-boats in her train;
On phantom-oars softly, the wind wavers by,
  Its dewy spray plashing my pane.
The midnight is scented with pine and new hay;
  A dreaming bird trills from her nest:
And—a letter to Gothamite Ned all the way
  From this lovely, too lovely, West.

Where are you? Abed, sir, and dreaming of me?
  Ah! at that old club, I dare say.
Or sweetly devoted to some horrid she,
  At an out-of-season soirée:
While poor little I sit as lone as a nun—
  Since Jim said good-night at the gate.
(As a rule, he comes in; but to-night, just for fun,
  We staid out too awfully late.)

We rode with a party, some twenty or more,
  All—this goes *sans dire*—two by two;—

IN THE ORIGINAL KEY.

(Three horses abreast make a ride just a bore,
  Jim told me, and so, once, did you!)
Rode out from the town, while the light died away,
  And tender dusk shrouded it round,
And soft dewdrops, like tears for the dead summer day,
  Grew and glistened along the ground.

We cantered, we trotted, we raced at our will,
  Winds fanning our cheeks as we sped;
The hush only broke by a bird's dreamy trill,
  Our horses' firm, resonant tread:
By "cricks" rippling gaily the roadside along,
  By cricket-chirps low on the green;
By the ring of our voices in laughter and song,
  The murmur of soft words between.

O poor city Ned! can't I make you just see
  The purple dusk sinking to night—
The baby-stars peeping out, winsome and wee,
  The moon drifting slowly in sight;
The long, shadowed road, with the grainfields beside,
  That billow like seas, in the wind,
Glinting fleets of gold ripples afloat on their tide
  In lights from the farms behind?

We passed corralled mares, looking wistfully out,
  With smooth noses over the wall;

IN THE ORIGINAL KEY.

And great mooing herds, that had put me to rout,
    If Jim had not scattered them all;
And queer little sheds with thatched roofs, where Jim said
    Small piggies were dreaming of mash—
And O, they are all little negro-pigs, Ned,
    With tails curled just like your mustache!

We came to a field, (or, as Jim says, a patch—)
    Where melons lay ripe for the knife;
And what did those boldest of boys, Ned, but snatch
    One apiece, and remount for dear life!
And quartered, and peeled, and ate turn-about bite
    By each two, it was really fun—
Though of course we pretended, we girls, that we *quite*
    Were shocked with the way they were won!

We ate apples, too; red and golden, Ned; gleaned
    From orchards we rode through at will;
And had lovely drinks from cold wells, intervened
    By cider new-drawn from the still.
And then we turned homeward, and raced score abreast
    To the depot and back again—
And I might have been winner — (Jim says I ride best —)
    But I was afraid of the train.

IN THE ORIGINAL KEY.

Then came the good-nights, and the verging of ways;
   And Neddie, the moon was so bright,
That when Jim proposed a ride down by the maize,
   I thought, just that once, that I might.
So we paced side by side, till houses were shut,
   And lights in the casements grew few,
And then, then—why, of course, dear, I took a short
    cut,
   And sped homeward to write to you!

So there it all is, a tale told to the end—
   And here is a kiss on the rim;
And now don't be cross, Ned, nor dare to pretend
   You are jealous of dear old Jim.
He, and more like him, sir, belong to my West,
   But somehow, the East calls me back,
To—O Neddie, your heart, dear, can read all the rest,
   Though not set down in white and black!

JIM.

THANKEE, Miss! I *will* set fur a spell, ef I may.—
 An' it's true thet to-morrer, ye're goin' away,
An' Pine Camps sees naught o' ye, arter terday?

Dern thet sun! It's so strong a chap's eyes can't but blink.—
These 'yer pines hez done well by ye, Miss, don't ye think? *
Fust-off, yer cheeks wuzn't so round nor so pink.

Clear four months, is it? No! Don't seem longer 'n one,
Sence thet stage thar, driv' up in th' settin' June sun,
An' yer little feet lit like birds on thet stun'.—

Got a chip on it 'yer—bruk it off thet same night!
Don't jest know, Miss, ez sech a poor chap hed a right,
But th' stars, lookin' on, blazed nary a mite—

An' I tho't thet yer eyes, bein' stars, too, ye see,
Might jest mebbe look soft ez them others on me,
Forgivin' a poor chap ez—love—med' too free.

IN THE ORIGINAL KEY.

Thar, it's out, an' thet's all; an' I'll bid ye goodby!
I jest sez ter mysel', "mek' a clean breast," sez I,
Fur 'taint in my line ter do aught on th' sly—

"An' then brave, like a man, say 'God bless ye,' an' go;
Which a-seein' yer love ain't fur bringin' her low,
She might mebbe rest her white hand in yer'n'"—so!

Thankee, Miss! Thet's a thing ez 'll last a chap's life!—
Now, good——God! thet word cuts thro' my heart like a knife.
Goodby!—Eh? Wot, love me? O Mary, my wife!

TRANSPLANTED.

A FRIEND o' her'n, I reckon? Wal, thar, jest ez I sed!
An' so she wouldn't hev' ye? An' now, poor child, she's dead,
An' sleepin' with her baby, terday, jest one sad year,
Beneath thet little gravestun', with lilies bloomin' near.

Thar, dear, set down an' rest ye. Ye're kinder tuckered out
With th' stretch from th' tavern, an' ye not over-stout.
Liked her a heap, I reckon? Th' man ez wants a wife,
Is bound ter git down peaky, an' out o' jint with life.

Jest let me change this apurn, an' set down fur a spell,
Seein' it's a long story ye're settin' me ter tell.—
Hey? O, she *war* short-merried, but a gal's life ain't told
By suns she's seen a-risin', nor jest th' years she's old!

Wal, two year kum this ploughin', she jined th' farm-house thar,
Merried ter young John Hardin', agin her mar an' par.
Sot on him she war sartin, an' loved him ter th' sky,
An' John war fine an' likely, tho' crankerty an' high.

IN THE ORIGINAL KEY.

She used ter tell me offen, ez how it kem about—
How thet fust summer 'yerways, when she war pestered out
With all th' city-courtin', an' finicky town-ways,
John fell like a wild-flower, inter her shet-up days.

She talked thet soft an' sweet-like, I used ter shet my eyes,
An' dream I heerd th' angels a-talkin' in th' skies.
When John set down th' figgers, an' brought her line so thin,
I think he might hev' reckoned her way o' talkin' in!

She told me how she loved him, he bein' big an' strong,
An' kinder cut fur helpin' sech little folks along.
How when his arms war roun' her, she felt like bird a-nest;
Jest foldin' her wings softly, an' cuddlin' down ter rest.

She war thet small an' tender, I think he jest swooped down,
An' took her up by power, afore she could look roun'.
Them Hardin's all was heighty, an' John th' top o' all,
An' love like thet jest pushes a woman ter th' wall.

Wal, fust John war ez happy ez enny man I seen;
Ez proud' an high an' mighty, ez tho' she war th' queen.
He didn't ask her nuthin', he gev' her all thar war,
An' wot she tho't war Scriptur', an' wot she sed war more.

IN THE ORIGINAL KEY.

So things went like June roses, a-bloomin' in th' sun,
Till John got his pride hurted, an' popped out like a gun;
She war *thet* dainty, allers, an' never ketched his ways,
An' seein' she knowed better, jest sot him in a blaze.

He allers liked John Hardin' th' best o' all th' lot,
An' when her manners shamed him, th' Hardin' pride got hot.
Ez much ez sech men ken love, he loved her et th' fust,
But when she riz his sperrit, she sot him et his wust.

Then she begun ter hanker, ez th' long months went by,
Fur th' old way o' livin', an' sometimes hed her cry;
An' tho' she allers hid it, John, he jest guessed th' hull,
An' took it hard an' ugly thet he war wearin' dull.

He didn't do much talkin', but jest got high an' stern;
Didn't mek' nuthin' o' her, pestered et ev'ry turn.
Wot‿e'er she done war crooked; wot she didn't, th' same,
An' it jest med' her dizzy, not bein' used ter blame.

So things went allers crosswise, an' they war allers out,
An' jest then kem a feller, an' kinder hung about—
Someun she'd knowed ter East'ards, thet told her o' her friends,
An' used her poor young feelin's all fur his own bad ends.

IN THE ORIGINAL KEY.

He stopped up ter th' tavern, an' gev' her most his days—
Sot him up fur a scholard, a-writin' up our ways;
He talked her par et mornin', he talked her mar et night,
An' sorter med' her reckon ez how he'd set things right.

Long-last, ter see his coat-tails, jest gev' poor John a spell—
Not thet he didn't trust her, a-knowin' her so well,
But they talked books an' music, an' set him et a loss,
An' riled him like a racer, ez kums in th' last hoss.

He got ter speak more sharper, ter show thet he allowed
He needn't know much po'try, ter not be easy cowed.
He wore his things more careless, an' put his manners by,
Ter prove thet he warn't shamefaced, afore a town-man's eye.

Wal, three months gone an' over, thet man, he gits a call
Ez how he must go East'ards, or jest go ter th' wall;
An' so he ups an' asks her, right in th' light o' day,
Ter quit her lawful husband, an' jine him on th' way.

Th' poor dear left him talkin', with nary look nor word;
Straight ez a streak o' lightnin', fast ez a frightened bird,
Kem ter me, 'yer, a-churnin', an' fell down weak an' white,
An' he jest took th' road thar, an' struck fur home. thet night.

IN THE ORIGINAL KEY.

I hetched up th' ole sorrel, an' went ter fetch in John,
Down in the weste'n medder, urgin' th' sowers on;
An' twixt us, she war kerried back ter her pretty room,
Whar birds sung et th' winders ter roses all in bloom.

Th' dizzy spell went off her, an' she kem slowly to;
An' when she seen John by her, a-lookin' strong an' true,
She jest war a new critter, an' set up in th' bed,
An' told him ev'ry wrinkle thet pesky man hed sed.

An' then, he sayin' nuthin', she jest took heart an' spoke
O' how they two warn't livin' bekumin' sech young folk—
How ef her failin's hurt him, 'twas unbeknownst, fur sure,
An' she knowed none amongst 'em, but his dear love 'ud cure.

She talked thet sweet an' lovin', I jest cried out my eyes,
A-hearin' how an angel war kumin' from th' skies—
A little baby-angel, ter take his mother's part,
An' give her back her nest-place within her husband's heart.

Then John, he kem out suddin, all in a burnin' flash.—
He "warn't ter be smoothed over by enny pritty trash.
Ef she'd hev' be'n th' woman ez his wife ought ter be,
Thet man hed hed his answer, afore he spoke so free.

IN THE ORIGINAL KEY.

He sed no word o' sinnin'—she hedn't heart fur thet—
Whoever drowndèd fur her, her feet 'ud not be wet!
He didn't take her whiteness ez enny keer fur him,
But thro' sin bein' water too rough fur her ter swim."

Thar warn't a thing from Adam not brought agin thet child;
I don't think John half meant 'em, but jest talked hisself wild.
An' top o' all kep' soundin' his tarnal, hurted pride
Thet he hed showed his failin's, a-stannin' by her side.

She heerd him white ez ashes, until his say war sed;
Then jest gev' one sob, soft like, an' trembled down in bed.
An' then God sent th' baby, ez drawed one little breath,
An' out o' life went driftin' back ter th' shore o' death.

Next day, ez shadders gethered, an' th' sun, goin' down,
Streamed in th' weste'n winders, a-givin' her a crown,
Ez red an' gold war fadin', she called John ter her bed,
An' looked up sweet an' lovin', an' jest then, she war dead.

We shet her blue eyes softly, an' smoothed her golden hair,
An' laid th' baby with her, an' parson sed a prayer;

IN THE ORIGINAL KEY.

An' soon th' two war lyin' in yonder little grave,
Whar birds sing sweet in summer, an' medder-lilies wave.

Thar, don't take on! She's happy, ef ever angel be.—
An' so she wouldn't hev' ye—an' ye right good ter see!
Wal, John he kinder took her, an' mebbe it war plann'd
How she war jest ter flower' ter be picked by his hand.

Eh? O, he took it hardly; leastways, fust-off, fur sure!
But John ain't jest th' natur' ter never find no cure.
He's courtin' Susan Tompkins, ez lives up th' Big Sainte—
A-goin'? Wal, I swanny! Ye *ain't* a-goin' ter faint!

BLACKBIRD.

SELL her? Sell my mare, this 'yer Blackbird?
'Yer, jest turn thet nag o' yern homewards,
    Or quit sharp! Skin *me*
Ef thet ain't th' barefacest sassin'!—
O Sal, Sal, I say! 'Yer's a swell 'yer,
Ez ups, marm, an' axes fur Blackbird
    From we.

Thet thar's my old woman, sir, thet is!
Fine figger, now, ain't she? Two hundred
    Is hern clear; thet's so.
Which same is all owin' ter Blackbird—
Ter this mare 'yer—(ho, thar, my beauty!)
Ez me an' Sal ain't et no loss fur
    Ter show.

Four years come this May, Sal an' me, sir,
Wuz spliced by th' parson, an' settled
    Up yon on Stagg's Pass;
Me billed fur Stagg's Mine; an' Sal chipper

IN THE ORIGINAL KEY.

Ez bird in her nest, in a shanty
I riz her o' pine, on a footin'
    O' grass.

A poor place enough it wuz, sartin!
Th' boys a rough lot, an' th' wimmin
    Cards o' th' same pack,
An' them thar red devils, th' Sioux,
Ez God, sir, hain't no hand in makin',
Ter right an' ter left o' us, sharp on
    Our track.

They took th' mines fust—broke th' shafts in,
An' undone th' work ez we'd be'n on
    Fur many a day;
Killed one chap ez bunked up th' mounting,
Stole hosses, an' then, et long last, sir,
Took one o' our decentest wimmin
    Away.

Et thet, up we riz—laid a trap, sir,
An' next night them sharps struck our diggin's,
    Thar wuz an explode;
An acc*i*dent—thet durned old powder
A-firin' itself, jest in time, sir,
Ter lay twenty Injuns in bits, on
    Th' road!

IN THE ORIGINAL KEY.

Then, jest fur a spell, all wuz quiet;
Us thar in th' Pass got right easy,
    An' all things went well,
Till one midnight, late thet same summer,
Ez suddin' ez lightnin' they struck us,
Strong by a round hundred, an' ragin'
    Ez hell!

Gosh! How things did rattle! Th' bar, sir,
Burned down ter th' ground, while them Injuns
    Got red-hot with drink;
An' out o' our doorway we seen 'em
A-ridin' our way with their torches
Jest blazin' like blood on th' night black
    Ez ink!

I didn't waste time, but shot out, sir,
Ter whar this 'yer Blackbird wuz corralled,
    An' bridled her smart;
Then Sal, ez wuz white ez yer shirt, thar,
Shinned up tight behind, an' we started,
Sal sobbin' a prayer ez kem straight from
    Her heart.

I ain't much in thet line myself, sir;
But thet night I prayed like a woman,
    Sal helpin' me on.

IN THE ORIGINAL KEY.

Ye see, it jest seemed thar wuz nuthin'
Else left fur a feller ter tackle—
An' ain't a last straw a durned better
    'N none?

I prayed, ez I sed; an' then stoopin'
Ter Blackbird, sez I, "Fly, fur God's sake!
    Fur life's sake, my Bird!"
An' thet mare jest doubled her paces,
With nary a whip nor a spur, sir,
An' flew like a critter ez minded
    My word.

Each step I tho't sure we wuz done fur.
Good Lord! Ef you'de seen th' road, stranger,
    We cleared et thet pace—
Sharp down th' sheer side o' a mounting,
Deep gullies along it, an' darkness
O' Egypt a-beatin' its wings in
    Our face!

Some ten mile ahead, thet road struck on
A settlement countin' some hundreds,
    Which same wuz my card;
But jest half-way thar wuz th' junction,
Our road strikin' plumb on th' trail, sir,

IN THE ORIGINAL KEY.

Them Injuns hed took from their diggin's,
    Mineward.

Thet one spot behind, we wuz saved, sir,
But Injuns is cute ez red Satan,
    An' does things up tight!
An' right from th' heart o' th' junction
A torch flickered up, an' on guard, sir,
A turn showed us plainly two Injuns
    In sight.

I pulled Bird up sharp, thinkin' mebbe
Ter lie low an' quiet, but blast 'em,
    Hoofs sounded behind!
They'd struck on our trail, an' wuz comin',
Th' hull pack o' hell-hounds, down on us,
.So Bird got her head, an' went on like
    Th' wind.

Ter hear them two sharps ez we neared 'em—
Sech whoopin'! Ye' see, in th' darkness
    Th' tellin' wuz rough
Who wuz an' who warn't o' their party,
An' doubt on them faces wuz funny;
But when th' light struck us, they fired
    Enough!

IN THE ORIGINAL KEY.

Sez I, "Sal, tain't no use; we're done fur!"
An' then a thought seizes me suddin',
    Ez how ter save her.
Sez I, "Sal, I'll fall when we strike 'em,
An—" Jest thar sez she: "Ez ye like, Dave,
But this 'yer old gal, she'll fall with ye,
    Yes, *sir!*"

'Twarn't no use ter argur. She gripped me,
An' waited; an' I, sir, ez knowed her
    Fur one o' her word,
Jest gev' us two up fur dead gone, sir:—
An' nearin' them two tarnal Injuns,
I'm comin', too, sir, ter th' story
    O' Bird.

Th' road wuz thet narrer ez them two
Took up pretty nigh its hull width, sir,
    With guns et full aim.
I gev' up fur lost, fur I knowed thet
No hoss could ride down them two varmints,
An' Blackbird wuz shy, an' not counted
    Jest game.

We wuzn't six yards from their faces—
Bang! bang! went th' guns, (an' one shot went
    Clean up this 'yer arm—)

IN THE ORIGINAL KEY.

An' then with a leap, we wuz flyin'
Along a clear road; them two Injuns
Behind on th' ground, an' us safe out
    O' harm.

Yes, *sir!* Her ez looks a poor critter,
Hed reasoned it out like a human,
    An' when th' pull kem,
(Which we thought she'd buck et a fence, sir,)
She jest gethered up on her haunches,
An' cleared them two Injuns, sir, flyin'—
    By Jem!

Thet's all, sir. Us two wuz th' only
Ones left o' th' thirty thet mined thar—
    Jest me an' my lass.
An' sence, we sunk shafts on th' Flat 'yer,
Not keerin' ter risk jest anuther
Sech night ez thet wuz, when we vamoosed
    Th' Pass.

So thet's how my Sal owes her hundreds
Ter this 'yer mare, crunchin' th' grass 'yer,
    An' why I wuz stirr'd
When ye axed ter bid fur her, stranger;
Fur her ez us owes our two lives to—
Fur her ez no money could buy—our
    Blackbird!

PIPES FROM OTHER PLACES.

A QUINTETTE OF SONG.

I.

LIFE.

A SONG of a White Throne circled
    By a girdle of white fire.—
Once on the flame God breathèd,
    Filled with divine desire.
Out, at His breath, there flickered
    A single tongue of flame,
Paling the golden planets,
    Putting the sun to shame.
It flashed thro' the flashing Saturn,
    It flamed thro' the flaming Mars,
Flooded the skies with glory,
    Glowed down the glowing stars;
Burst on the six-day Eden,
    And since has the world been rife
With fruit of that flame from heaven—
    The God-breathèd flame of Life.

PIPES FROM OTHER PLACES.

II.

LOVE.

A SONG of a wondrous garden
    Far up the sky's still height,
Glowing with Eden lilies,
    And roses of virgin white—
Lightly the rare bloom over,
    An angel, once, wandering,
The fairest rose in the garden
    Brake with her trailing wing.
It fell thro' a rift in heaven,
    And bounded from star to star;
Bruising its soft stem sorely
    Over the sky's gold bar—
Sank to the world all crimson
    With wounds, and the scars thereof
Are the thorns we feel, who bosom
    The ruddy, warm rose of Love.

PIPES FROM OTHER PLACES.

III.

SONG.

A SONG of a harp in heaven
    That swept by a seraph-wing,
Once from its stirred chords loosened
    A note from a single string.—
It trembled out heaven's portal,
    Waking the hush of space:
Stole down the skies at midnight,
    Laughed as the winds gave chase:
It echoed along the chamber
    Of silent and viewless air,
To gate of the world of mortals,
    And lingered in wonder there;
Till an unborn soul, in passing,
    Bore it unto life along,
And so to the world was wafted
    The heaven-born soul of Song.

PIPES FROM OTHER PLACES.

IV.

PEACE.

A SONG of a fair young angel
    At the gold gate of heaven.—
Her eyes in twin-stars, serenely
    Shone thro' the veil of even;
Her wings played as light and softly
    As clouds down the empty sky;
Her breath thro' the scented twilight
    In a zephyr floated by.
Her white hands were folded meekly;
    Grave sweetness was on her face;
She plucked a plume from her bosom,
    And wafted it down thro' space—
And she sang "O world, but wear it,
    And thy strife and fray shall cease!"
For the plume from the angel's bosom
    Was the angel's gift of Peace.

PIPES FROM OTHER PLACES.

V.

DEATH.

A SONG of a treasure chamber
    Set high against heaven's door.—
Unfinished crowns strew brightly
    Portal and walls and floor.
One for each man and woman
    Striving on earth, is there;—
Pearls for the pure in spirit,
    Rubies for deed and prayer.
Angels fashion them daily;
    Each as it falls complete,
A cherub gathers up fondly,
    And bears to the Judgment-Seat;
Thence, at God's bidding, seeks one
    Weary of mortal breath,
And lays on the pale, wan forehead,
    The crown that we christen Death.

CLEO.

(C. D.)

HAD I the choosing of her days,
   There were no skies too fair for her;
No suns too bright to gild her ways,
No song too sweet to sing her praise;
   Nor bloom too rich, too rare for her,
Had I the choosing of her days.

Had I the choosing of her nights,
   No purple dusk were meet for her;
No moon too gold on twilight heights,
No stars too fraught of silver lights;
   Nor dream too warm, too sweet for her,
Had I the choosing of her nights.

Had I the choosing of her years,
   May could not bud too oft' for her;—
No June too crowned of rose-red spheres,
No Fall of tinted wolds and meres;

PIPES FROM OTHER PLACES.

Nor snows too white, too soft for her,
Had I the choosing of her years.

Had I the choosing of her life,
   No bliss were great for her desert;
Her joyous hours, unknown to strife,
Should be of love and laughter rife;
   Nor woe should wound, nor blight should hurt,
Had I the choosing of her life.

Had I the choosing of her love,
   There were no heart too pure for her;
Whose love her's crowned, should first disprove
Self, sin, and all the stains thereof;
   Strong to live, die, endure for her,
Should be my choosing of her love!

How has she grown so to my heart?
   Why does my love so cling to her?
She is all sweet, all pure of art—
She has no peer, no counterpart.
   Sing soft, my song, to sing to her,
Who has so grown unto my heart!

Her face is dusky as the night,
   And shades of gloaming haunt her hair;

PIPES FROM OTHER PLACES.

Her eyes are stars of liquid light,
And pure as moonshine, drift in sight
　The tides that color rich and rare
Her face that dusky is as night.

She goes her way with simple grace,
　She has the calm of a young queen
Born of a long and noble race.
Pride sits with sweetness on her face;
　And stateliness does mark her mien,
Who goes her way with simple grace.

But grace nor beauty makes her dear,
　As dear she is to all who know;
For her young soul, more blithe, more clear
Than April stream that seeks the meer—
　Her tender heart, white, pure as snow,
For these, who know her hold her dear.

Hence has she grown close to my heart,
　Hence does my true love cling to her,
And yearn to save her sin and smart,
To hold her from all blight apart;
　Hence pray I, (while I sing to her—)
" God wear thee close within His Heart."

AFTER THE BALL.

O LITTLE glove, do I but dream I hold thee,
    So warm, so sweet, and tawny as her hair?
Nay! from her hand to-night I dared unfold thee,
    As we went down the stair.

She said no word; she did not praise nor blame me;
    She is so proud, so proud and cold and fair!—
Ah! dear my love, thy silence did not shame me,
    As we went down the stair.

Thy dark eyes flashed; thy regal robes arrayed thee
    In queenly grace, and pride beyond compare;
But on thy cheek a sudden red betrayed thee,
    As we went down the stair.

O, lady mine, some near night will I prove thee!
    By this soft glove I know that I may dare
Take thy white hand, and whisper, "Sweet, I love thee,"
    As we go down the stair!

THREE SERENADES.

I.

THE sunbeams are sleeping
    Under the hill;
Over the gloam plains the whippoorwill;
Pale dreams the lily on rocking lake,
Slumber the ferns in their maiden brake.
    Tender as prayer
    Croons the languid breeze,
A lullaby for the nodding trees;
And under the sheen of grasses green
    The violet is sleeping.
        Where—where—
O my belovèd, sleepest thou?

The young stars sail shyly
    Out of the dark,
Drifting in wake of the moon's gold bark.

PIPES FROM OTHER PLACES.

Wakens the rose with a scented sigh,
As rustling robe of the wind sweeps by.
    Bird in the fen
    Calls bird in the tree,
As wave calls wave on the flowing sea;
And white to her mate, compassionate,
    The dove is coming shyly.
      When—when—
O my belovèd, comest thou?

II.

    My shy love, my sweet love,
      I sing to thine eyes.—
O blue seas, flow gently beneath thy lashed skies!
Thy deep tides abreast, with nor rudder nor chart,
To Scylla of love, as a spar drifts my heart.—
O blue seas, flow gently beneath thy lashed skies!
    I sing, O my sweet love,
      I sing to thine eyes!

    My fond love, my fair love,
      I sing to thy lips.—
O rose-leaves, unfold thee thy dewy red slips!
A captive my soul thy twin blushes between—

PIPES FROM OTHER PLACES.

(Ah! sweeter my bondage than freedom, I ween.)
O rose-leaves, unfold thee thy dewy red slips!
    I sing, O my fair love,
        I sing to thy lips!

    My proud love, my pure love,
        I sing to thy heart.—
O white bird, I hold thee—thou may'st not depart!
Thou plumest thy wings, and thou strivest to flee,
But fetter of love binds thee fast unto me.—
O white bird, I hold thee—thou may'st not depart!—
    I sing, O my pure love,
        I sing to thy heart!

III.

Slumbers the sun in the twilight west,
Lamb in the fold, and bird in the nest.
Slumberest thou, O love loveliest?—
    While I woo thee,
Star smiles to star in the sky's abyss,
And pulsing, paling, with might of bliss,
The blue sea drinks of the moon's white kiss.—
    Wilt thou kiss me?

Along the sweep of the dark morass,
Where gentle winds on linked pinions pass,

PIPES FROM OTHER PLACES.

There sounds the sigh of the lonely grass.—
    I sigh for thee.
Across the hush of the aspen vale
There echoes plaint of a nightingale
Whose fickle mate his love does fail.—
    Wilt thou fail me?

No more, no more, sing I sky or sea
Of sun or star, or of bird on tree.
O love, forever my song shall be
    Of thee, of thee!
Whose face than lily is fairer far;
Whose heart is pure as the angels are;
Who art all, all—sun, song, and star
    To me, to me!

BY THE RIVER.

ROCKED by soft winds that down the sunshine blow
    From high, cool mountains to its gentle tide,
  Where anchored fleets of white-sailed lilies ride,
A river, cradled erst in Alpine snow.
Here, like an unled child, who fears to go
    Or on or back, it frets from side to side,
  Till sea-born Thetis, glowing as a bride,
Lures with wet lips to nuptial caves below.

Sweetheart, thou art all new to life and love,
And fearful of the deep tides loosed thereof;
  A fleet of lilies are thy maiden dreams,
At anchor still within thy calm young breast;
Love calls! and shyly out at his behest
  Thou comest, white as bloom of Alpine streams!

FALL HARBINGERS.

NO green around the wayside stone,
    No song upon the tree;
Across the dark the night-winds moan,
    And shudder to the sea.

No moon within the empty sky;
    The starless air is chill;
And silently the sad mists lie
    Like phantoms on the hill.

O dreary wold! O darksome night!
    O brown and barren lea!
O pine upon thy lonely height!
    O wind of the white sea!—

Not thine, not thine alone, the wail
    That telleth of the Fall;—
One winsome face grown cold and pale—
    This, this, hath told me all!

ON THE HILL.

(A LITTLE old house on a hill.
    Dark behind,
The tall pines; and before,
The white drift of sea to the shore.

Across the night-shadows, the trill
    Of a bird;
And the tender and sweet
Love-sigh of the grass at my feet.)

O little old house on the hill!
    Dear of yore
Thy mossed gables to me;
Thy gate, and thy path's greenery—

Thy threshold, cool, shadowed and still;
    And above,
In a tangled, bright vine,
Thy roses, and sweet eglantine.

PIPES FROM OTHER PLACES.

O little old house on the hill!
      Lone and pale
Thou art haunted to-day,
By phantoms of youth fled for aye;—

Of dreams life shall never fulfill—
      Dreams of love,
That are proven, ah, me!
Chill, empty, and vain utterly.

O little old house on the hill!
      One there was—
(Was? Ah, heart, learn to bear!)
Once light on thy threshold and stair;—

Once peeping, rose-like, o'er thy sill—
      One whose voice
With the birds' rang in tune,
Whose smile was sweet, glowing as June.

O little old house on the hill!
      Where is she,
Who in sunshine and snow
Here dwelt in the years long ago?

Beyond the wide sea, and the shrill
      Cry of winds,

PIPES FROM OTHER PLACES.

One hath borne her afar,
And high above us, as yon star.

O little old house on the hill!
    Sweet her eyes;
And how fragrant and fair
The rippled gold float of her hair.—

Doth love in her heart hold us still?
    "Nay?"—The night,
How it darks and grows chill—
O little old house on the hill!

THE DESERTED CHAPEL.

A CHAPEL by the wayside,
    Silent, and dark, and chill;
Out of the gloom, and the solemn hush,
The plaintive notes of a lonely thrush,
    And wail of whippoorwill.

White on the untrod threshold,
    Daisies in virgin file;
While stately grasses troop up in green,
And scaling the steps that intervene,
    Fade in the dusky aisle.

Silent, within the belfry,
    A bell with shattered tongue;
And swallows twit in the chancel eaves
Where wild vines clamber, and twine their leaves
    The warm brown nests among.

O chapel by the wayside,
    Sad tales thy ruins tell!
Out of thy shadows pale phantoms dart—

PIPES FROM OTHER PLACES.

Out of thy silence strange echoes start,
    O mute old iron bell!

  Again the weary pilgrims
    Thine aisles tread, as of yore;
Again the toll, and the measured tread
Of patient mourners, who bear their dead
    Without thy shadowed door.

  Again the pealing organ,
    The roses down thy nave;
The laughing bells, and the happy bride,
Who saw not lying the year beside,
    This tiny, moss-grown grave.

TO THE RAIN.

WHENCE, silver rain, and wherefore? O, bare us all thine heart!
Of all God's mute evangels, most pure, most dear, thou art.
        No friend thou, of fair weather,
        To flee when shadows gather,
        And golden days grow drear;
But where the gloom falls darkest, there straightway dost appear,
On wings of wind down-sinking from some seraphic sphere!

As veiled nuns, meek and holy, down still cathedral aisle,
From heaven's shadowed cloister, mists follow in dark file;
        And in sweet stave and quaver,
        As thy light pinions waver
        In mystic rhythms from high,
The silent air, responsive, its voice lifts tunefully,
In zephyr-incensed chorals that echo to the sky.

PIPES FROM OTHER PLACES.

In vain the lightnings fold thee, fierce thunders press thy
    wake;
In vain the wrathful whirlwinds thy swift flight overtake.
        Fail thou dost not, nor falter,
        Till priest-like, from earth's altar,
        Thine hour consummated,
Back to thy shrine thou goest, on wings of sweet air sped,
And bow of heaven encircled to aureole thy head.

All nature names thee high-priest, and greets with humble
    knee;
No king-tree in proud forest, annointed not by thee.
        No queen-rose of the bower,
        But meekly as field-flower
        Doth crave thy fragrant chrism;
Anunciation-lilies bend white for thy baptism—
Alone are men defiant of thine evangelism!

Yet, true to thy high mission, turned not from thine intent,
Year upon year thou pourest thy cleansing sacrament.
        Pure as the manna given
        White once, from open heaven;
        Sweet as the nard of old;
And eloquent all mutely of Him the skies enfold,
Whom but the pure in spirit are promised shall behold.

PIPES FROM OTHER PLACES.

O silver rain, we know thee! Thine heart faith layeth bare.
Thou figurest the hyssop whence our soiled souls rise fair.
   Tears, tears alone may purge them,
   Whence they shall pure emerge them
   Of all that stains them now,
As from thy ministration, erst sullied lilies glow.—
In hyssop of contrition, Lord, wash us white as snow!

THE WIND.

ETERNAL wind, I know thee!
   Thou art some hapless sprite,
Once by a rift in heaven,
   Tempted to earthward flight.
The little rift closed over,
   Ope'd not to thy soft wing;
Now—nor of earth nor heaven—
   Thou plainest, wandering:
Beatest thy wings in sorrow,
   Weepest sad tears of rain,
Wooest from heaven's shut portal
   Shadows, in mournful train.
Only wooest the sunshine,
   When, with thy golden strain,
Singing of wondrous heavens
   Never thine own again.

Ever thy gladdest carol
   Diest in this refrain—

PIPES FROM OTHER PLACES.

"Never, alas! ah, never,
   Never mine own again!"—
Why do we list and love thee
   Most in thy minor strain—
Why do our mute hearts echo
   Thy yearning and thy pain?
Ah! in what human bosom
   Beatest a heart so blest,
But yearnest some lost heaven
   Of love, or faith, or rest?—
But knowest some kin exile,
   And with thee, wind, dost plain,
"Never, alas! ah never,
   Never mine own again!"

A SNOW-SONG.

SNOWFLAKES, snowflakes, fleet and fair,
  Pray ye, your sweet secret share!
Are ye come by fate or chance,
In your virgin radiance?
Stars are ye from the White Throne—
Birds from paradise new-flown—
Sparks from Mary's aureole—
Pure prayers seeking a pure soul—
Crumbs of manna—crystals fine,
Chalicing Christ's altar-wine—
Lilies from the Eden bloom—
Flax from off swift Martha's loom—
Feathers from the happy flight
Of young angels, winged and white—
Grace-notes from the divine strain
Cherubs chant in long refrain—
White souls waiting mortal birth,
Becked by baby-hands to earth—
Sweet, wet kisses from the sky—
Pearls from out God's treasury—

PIPES FROM OTHER PLACES.

Letters from our holy dead—
Spray from limpid Lethe shed—
Fairy boats with sails unfurled,
Wrecked on reef of our harsh world—
Darts from Cupid, gaily sent
Out his bow with fond intent—
Foam from champing coursers bound
In the Happy Hunting Ground—
Truce-flags of the warring skies—
White lids for blue crocus-eyes—
Virgin loves of the cold wind—
Maiden hearts left still unshrin'd—
Vague, vain dreams of wistful youth—
Angel-tears for human ruth—
Ariels in mystic quest—
Plumes from out the phœnix-breast—
Censors swung at Mary's shrine—
Flakes of incense, rich as wine—
Scattered leaves from angel-lore—
Sands from Charon's farther shore—
Unsung songs of cadence dumb
Till the bidden singers come—
Poems that wait the chosen lyre—
Flames from God's white altar-fire?
Pray ye, pray ye, share with me,
Snowflakes, your white mystery!

THE LESSON OF THE CRUCIFIX.

DOES thy heart in some Gethsemane
    Quail as the chalice nears?
Art worn and weary beneath thy cross
    Of anguished years?
Does thy soul shrink from the Calvary
    Death beckest fast?
O learn of the Crucifix to love
    What pain thou hast!

Does thy bare brow yearn the laurel crown,
    Or bay that hailest Fame?
Or long for the wreath of roses red
    That Love acclaim?
The Brow drooped low on the cruel Cross,
    What crown adorns?
O learn of the Crucifix to love
    Thy crown of thorns!

Are thy hands weary of endless work,
    That winnest thee no gain?

PIPES FROM OTHER PLACES.

Do they yearn the fold, the tender clasp
    Of friend, in vain?
The dear Hands stretched on the cruel Cross,
    The sharp nail brands.
O learn of the Crucifix to love
    Thine empty hands!

Do thy feet falter and weakly fail,
    Pressing the narrow way?
Are they sore-wounded with thorns and tares,
    From day to day?
The dear Feet nailed to the cruel Cross—
    Was Their way sweet?
O learn of the Crucifix to love
    Thy wounded feet!

Is thy heart yearning in vain, in vain,
    The love that others know?
Is its faith wasted, its trust betrayed,
    Its dream laid low?
See in the Heart on the cruel Cross
    Its counterpart,
And learn of the Crucifix to love
    Thy lonely heart!

For be thou lover of Christ in truth,
    Thou will'st not pain forswear;

PIPES FROM OTHER PLACES.

But lone Olivet and Calvary
    Glad with Him share.
For thee hast He borne His Agony,
    For thee His Death—
Then murmur not, tho' thou shar'st His Cross
    To thy last breath!

Not to far lands must thou go in search,
    The Cross with Him to bear.
Take but bravely up thy daily task,
    Thy common care.
Breast brave and meekly the thorns in life
    So sorely sown,
And He shall not on the lonely Cross
    Be nailed alone!

A Via Crucis the world to all,
    Of high or humble part;
No life exempt from the cross that waits
    Hands, feet and heart.
Yet, falter not—to the end be firm,
    And Christ beside,
In Paradise shalt thy cross turn crown,
    O crucified!

A VIRGIN CHAPLET.

QUEEN of the Holy Rosary,
    I kneel before thy shrine,
Within my hands the little beads that tell me child of
    thine.

And as the decades, one by one,
    I thread with Aves sweet,
My soul another chaplet weaves, to lay at thy dear feet;—

The chaplet of my girlish life,
    Strung on the golden chain
Of glad young years like outposts bright, of riper life's
    gray fane.

And O, though all unworth thy meed.
    I pray thou wilt impart
A blessing on the rosary I bead thee with my heart!

First of the decades name I Faith
    In thy virginity,
That all immaculate, yet riped to pure maternity.—

PIPES FROM OTHER PLACES.

(To Father, Son, and Holy Ghost,
All glory be for aye,
Who hailed thee bless'd forever on Annunciation-Day!)

The second decade pleads my Hope
That thy dear Son may be
Forgiving to my wayward soul, that pardon prays thro' thee.—

(To Father, Son, and Holy Ghost
All glory be for aye,
Who hope embodied for the world, on thy Conception-Day!)

The decade third I bead with Deeds,
Past, present, and to be.
Tho' all below thy Son's high worth, O, offer them for me!—

(To Father, Son, and Holy Ghost,
All glory be for aye,
Who proved thee priestess of mankind on the first Christmas-Day!)

With Love is strung the decade fourth—
Love human and divine;
Fan thou my love of God to flame—the human, purge, refine!—

PIPES FROM OTHER PLACES.

    (To Father, Son, and Holy Ghost,
      All glory be for aye,
Who named thee our meek model on Purification-Day!)

    Last is the decade of my Prayers
      For soul's and body's need.
My Mother, Christ will not deny, if thou but intercede.—

    (To Father, Son, and Holy Ghost,
      All glory be for aye,
Who intercessor at the Throne, crowned thee, Assumption-Day!)

    Queen of the Holy Rosary,
      Maid, mother, undefiled,
This chaplet of her soul accept from thine unworthy child.

    And as the decades, one by one,
      The swift years shall complete,
O, up the beads, as stepping-stones, guide me to thy Son's Feet!

A LAMP FOR THE TABERNACLE.

DEAR Lord, a little lamp I bring
    To burn before Thy shrine;
No gold nor jeweled offering,
    But red and warm as wine.

The taper is but newly lit,
    Yet cast it not away;
In love adoring pledge I it
    Thine ever, from this day.

Thro' sun and cloud, thro' light and shade,
    Thro' dawn, and dusk, and night,
Thro' pain that stays, and joys that fade,
    Thro' blee and bitter blight—

I bid it glow more warm, more red,
    With each brief passing hour,
As a pale bud is ripenèd
    Into a ruddy flower.

PIPES FROM OTHER PLACES.

And as its flames shall upward wreathe
    By midnight, and by day,
I bid its faithful taper breathe
    A sweeter incense aye—

That when life, like a failing flame,
    Shall fade to death away,
Still Thine may be the heart I name
    Thy votive lamp, to-day.

ADIEU.

A DIEU! To God!
    In all love's mystic language
No word so sweet as this,
Wherein some dear, dear heart to God we tender
    Between the sob and kiss.

    No song, no poem,
    No prayer, has its completeness,
      Its pathos, faith, its love;—
Not one on earth is meet to guard our treasure—
    Meet only Him above!

    O hearts! O lips!
    Not for the common parting
      Where no love is, nor pain—
Not for the farewells spoken 'mid light laughter,
    This holy word profane:

    But hold in trust
    For life's sure Passion-hour,
      When scourging fates beset,

PIPES FROM OTHER PLACES.

And called our souls, to tender their best lovèd
On Parting's Olivet.

O sundered breasts!
O sore souls torn and bleeding!
O lonely hearts that ache!
Love is a bond earth's partings forge but firmer,
Nor death itself shall break.—

And each "A Dieu,"
As from faint lips it falters,
Has issue great and grand,
Our dear ones shrining surely in the Hollow
Of God's own guarding Hand.

TO MY CRITICS.

I PRAY you hear my song of a bird,
  My song of a bird fledged newly;
She plumed her wings on a sunny day,
And flew to the far, free west away,
  To mountains misted bluely:—

To heights that cloister the virgin snows,
  To canyons by cool brooks purlèd;
To hills that warden the vale's retreats,
To grass-seas ridden by flower-fleets,
  With petal-sails unfurlèd.

When back one even', on homeward wing,
  She fluttered with long flight weary,
To kindred sheltered their nests among,
She shyly lilted a glad young song
  Of mountain and of eyrie:—

Of twilight woods with their scents of pine,
  Of the rose that rides the prairie;

CODA.

*Of still ravines where the cactus hides,
And rivers timing their rippled tides
  To the west wind's vagary.*

*The wise birds listed her simple lay,
  And sang, " She is joyous, truly.
Her prelude-pipes soar no note above
The scale of youth, but she sings for love—
  We will not carp unduly!"*

*So the bird sang on, and year by year
  More strong rose her song, and sweeter.—
O critics mine! may I pray you be
So kind as my fabled birds, to me,
  Whose voice is new to meter?*

www.ingramcontent.com/pod-product-compliance
Lightning Source LLC
Chambersburg PA
CBHW020054170426
43199CB00009B/282